TALL TALES

Volume 13

Tales of the Wild West Series

Rick Steber

Illustrations by Don Gray

D1016454

NOTE
Tall Tales is the thirteenth book in the
Tales of the Wild West Series

Tall Tales
Volume 13
Tales of the Wild West Series

Bonanza Publishing
Box 204
Prineville, Oregon 97754

INTRODUCTION

A tall tale begins innocently with convincing facts and a few trivial details thrown in. But in the course of the story the limits of believability are stretched to the breaking point. In the end we are left wondering how we could have been so naive, so darn gullible.

America's tall tales have been handed down through generations and are firmly rooted in character, situation and landscape. In the past a skillfully-told yarn was a diversion from the drudgery and monotony of everyday life and tellers of tall tales were held in high regard because their stories made people laugh.

A tall tale is best enjoyed when told aloud. Dialect, intonation and gestures add to the story. A pause here. A shake of the head there. A practiced laugh. A wink, a sly smile or a deadpan look provide seasoning and can communicate as much as a well-placed word.

In our modern fast-paced world, dominated by instant communication, changing technology and constant entertainment, the tall tale is no longer considered an essential part of everyday life. As a result, the telling of tall tales has become a dying art form.

BIG FISH STORY

"Biggest fish I ever landed was in 19 'n' 38. Remember it like it was yesterday," lied the old fisherman.

"Grasshoppers were as thick as hair on a hound dog's back. I was using a hopper for bait and to be perfectly honest I was taking a little snooze when all of a sudden my rod is nearly jerked out of my hand. I grab it, rear back and set the hook. But my line busts. I lose the fish.

"I take a spool of heavy line, string it on my reel, tie on a hook, slip a lively hopper into place and throw back out in the same spot. This time I'm not sleepy 'cause I figure I got a big fish in a hungry way.

"Sure enough, he takes the bait. But he also takes my rigging and strips off every inch of line. I vow then and there to catch that doggone monster. I run back to town, buy a hundred feet of one-inch hemp rope and have the blacksmith fashion me a hook from a double-ought horse shoe.

"When I get to my fishing hole I bait up with the biggest hopper I can find, throw in and tie off to the top of a fair-sized tree. Just before dark I catch that fish. He fights terrible hard and since there ain't nothing I can do I go home, come back the next morning and that tree is still whipping back and forth. It took two full days for that fish to finally tire. Then I hired a team of stout horses to pull it up on the bank.

"I can't rightly recite how big that fish was in yards and feet but to show you — a logging outfit ended up suing me. They were having a log drive at the time and when I pulled that fish out they claimed it dropped the river level so much there wasn't enough water to float their logs."

MOTHER-IN-LAW

A man bought a small piece of ground and tried to scratch a living by farming and trading horses on the side. But truth was, he did not have much of an eye for horse flesh and as a result lost more money than he made.

Take the time a traveler was passing through the country and pawned a horse on him. On the surface the horse, a bay with a blaze that ran the length of his nose, was well fed and seemed to have a good disposition. But one morning he was standing in the corral pretending to sleep, eyes closed, one hind hoof tipped. The homesteader, carrying a bucket of grain, passed behind and the bay suddenly came to life, kicking out with deadly force. The pail went flying and the man grabbed at his bleeding wrist.

After that, every time any living creature came near, the horse kicked. The homesteader made up his mind to get rid of the bay. But word had quickly circulated and none of his neighbors wanted to trade.

"I've got no choice but to put that ornery outlaw down," the homesteader told his wife. While he was making this announcement his mother-in-law, who had come for a visit, wandered into the barnyard and was kicked in the head. She died the next day.

At her funeral a number of men from out of town gathered and someone commented to the homesteader, "I see a lot of friends came quite a distance for the funeral."

"They're not friends," said the homesteader.

"Well then, what are they doing here?"

"After the funeral I'm gonna be auctioning off that bay. I suppose they're all men who have a mother-in-law."

3

LIAR

One hot summer day a stranger appeared in the Pastime Tavern, slid a dime down the bar and instructed the bartender, "Bring me a cold one."

When the bartender brought the beer the stranger tried to engage him in small talk about the weather, the price of grain and, very casually, about fishing and hunting prospects around those parts.

"I wouldn't know," shrugged the bartender. Then he nodded toward the other end of the bar to where a husky man, the only other customer in the joint, sat hunched over a nearly empty glass of beer. "Buy Casey a round. He'll tell you everything you want to know about fishing and hunting."

The stranger took a seat next to Casey and inquired, "If a fellow was in the mood for fishing, where could he go?"

"Most anywhere," replied Casey. "The government got the season closed but that don't matter none to us locals. Why just the other day I reeled me in a real nice fish. In fact, I measured him and he went 14 inches."

"That's not so big," said the stranger.

"Depends on how you measure," claimed Casey. "Around here we measure between the eyes."

"Oh," was all the stranger was able to say. After a moment he inquired, "Do you ignore the hunting season, too?"

"Of course," replied Casey. "We don't pay attention to seasons, bag limits or the manner in which fish and game can be taken. Why, just this morning I killed a deer, three grouse, two swans and a bald eagle."

The stranger yanked his wallet from a hind pocket and flipped it open to expose a shiny badge. "Allow me to introduce myself, I'm the new game warden."

And Casey replied, "Allow me to introduce myself. I'm the biggest liar this side of Denver."

NED THE CARP

The cowboy began to spin a windy. "The most favorite pet I ever had in my life was a fish. To be precise — a carp.

"I became acquainted with that carp after hooking him while fishing for trout. I figured it best to get a trash fish like that out of the river and so I tossed him up on the bank. But in nothing flat he was at my feet and so I tossed him again and this time I watched and I'll be doggone if he didn't flip himself up on his tail and walk to me.

"After that I lost interest in fishing and climbed on my horse and rode toward the bunkhouse three miles away. When I got there I told the other buckaroos my story and they thought it was the funniest thing they ever heard. But the laughter died straight-away when I opened the door and that fish came strolling in like he owned the joint.

"'He's here ta stay so you're gonna have ta come up with a name for him,' claimed one of the buckaroos.

"I shrugged because I sure as heck didn't have a name for a carp that done followed me home.

"'Call him Ned,' suggested one of the men. 'I had an uncle name of Ned that looked just about like him.'

"And so Ned stuck. Ned became a scenic attraction and folks from miles around came to have a look. One of these visitors was a fiddle player and before the evening was out we ended up having a dance. You guessed it, the best dancer of the whole dang outfit was Ned. He was a wonder doing dizzy spins, somersaults and end-for-end flips.

"Ned refused to leave my side. He followed me everywhere — to the barn, when I moved cows, around the field when I mowed hay. One day he followed me onto a little footbridge that crossed over the creek. I'll be darned if that fish didn't slip, fall in the water and before I could pull him out, he drowned."

ASTRAL KID

"The lure of gold attracts many strange characters," said J.A. Riley, a prospector in the Silver Peak region of Nevada when gold was discovered in 1907. "But the strangest of all was Bob Rohane. He came drifting in saying that spirits from another world had directed him to stake his claim up on the side of a nearby hill. With talk like that we soon tagged him with the nickname Astral Kid.

"The Astral Kid spent many days carving a trail, which he called the Spirit Walk, around the hillside, grooming the trail with a nail-toothed rake. He built a telephone line, sinking stakes into the ground and stringing wire along the top. He claimed this allowed him to communicate directly with the spirit world. At the head of this trail he sank a tunnel. Eventually it extended 150 feet into the side of the hill.

"Having the Astral Kid in camp gave us plenty of diversion in the long winter evenings because at the drop of a hat he would put himself into a trance, claiming he was flying forth in an astral journey. After a few moments he began speaking, telling us in great detail of exotic ports of call such as Honolulu, Melbourne and Hong Kong. Invariably he would meet a woman of captivating charms and we would hang on every word of his vivid descriptions. Why, it was the next best thing to actually spending a night in town."

One day the Astral Kid suddenly departed, saying the spirits had told him to abandon his claim and directed him to a place miles away where pay dirt lay closer to the surface. He walked away from the camp and never returned.

Years later a rich vein was discovered below the Astral Kid's original claim and the Spirit Mine produced a fortune for its new owners.

JUMP

This story occurred during the early days of flying. A traveling barnstormer came through the country offering to give townfolks a ride for a buck.

A young man paid his dollar and in return the pilot gave him a pack. "What is it?" the kid wanted to know. "A parachute," he was told. "Strap it on your back. If we get in trouble and I tell you to jump, I want you to count to three and pull this cord. Pull it hard."

The young man strapped on the parachute, crawled into the passenger seat and readied himself for takeoff. The engine roared, the propeller blew wind and smoke in his face and they raced along the bumpy ground. Then they were in the air flying smoothly and the young man opened his eyes and looked.

Below were horses and cows looking small and distant. He saw a thin, twisting ribbon of river and the swimming hole where kids gathered during the hot summer months and swung on a rope before dropping into the deep water. There was the hill behind his house, the home place, his sister in the front yard waving her arms.

They continued on until suddenly the engine lost a beat, belched black smoke and the nose of the plane dropped. All was quiet except for the whistling wind. The pilot yelled, "Jump!"

The young man did as he was told. He remembered the instructions and diligently counted, "One — two — three," and pulled the rip cord. Nothing happened. The ground was rushing to meet him. He looked between his legs and noticed a man hurtling upward and as they neared the young man shouted, "Do you know anything about parachuting?"

They passed and the other man hollered, "No. Do you know anything about Coleman stoves?"

MY BEAR HUNT

The old man was sitting in the tavern on the first seat at the bar. A tenderfoot wandered in and the old man grabbed him by the sleeve and implored, "Sit down here, friend. I ever tell you about the time I went bear hunting?

"Well, it was in the fall. There had already been a dusting of snow in the high country. You probably know this, but just before bears go into hibernation they are as fat and sassy as they get. That is the best time to hunt bear.

"I crawled on Scout, my saddle horse. He was as trusty a critter as ever walked on four feet. I packed many a deer and elk and bear with him. But anyways, back to my bear hunt. I went riding off on Scout into the hills, went a considerable long ways before I caught sight of a bear. From the size I judged him to be a two-year-old. He was so preoccupied in trying to dig a squirrel out from under a tree root that he never even suspected I was in the county.

"I kilt him, field-dressed him where he lay and with a great amount of exertion succeeded in loading the beast on Scout. As it turned out that was the easy part because on the way back we had to ford a river. Maybe I failed to mention this but Scout was plumb terrified of water. Still, I'm thinking with a little encouragement I can coax him to cross. But Scout absolutely refused.

"And so finally I pull the bear off, balance it over my shoulders and stagger into the river. Not to brag none but in those days I was big and strong as an ox. Still, it seemed that bear weighed a solid ton. I had to walk the bottom, came up coughing and sputtering and as I crawled out on the far bank I took a look and dang it all — that horse of mine was riding atop of the bear. Really did happen. Yeah, I swear it did.

"So, I ever tell you about the time...."

9

AMAZING

The first white baby born west of the Mississippi River was the son of Hiram and Minnie Jones. A moment after he reached this world Hiram whispered to his wife, "He's something special. He's going to be a great, great man." Because of Hiram's intuition he insisted the baby be given the name Amazing, Amazing Jones. But as the child grew there was nothing that set him apart from the other pioneer children. He never won the spelling bee. He was never the star of the Christmas play. He was not a good aim.

Years passed. Amazing Jones married a local girl and upon the birth of their first child, a son, he told his wife, "I could never name him after myself. All my life this name has been an albatross around my neck. I feel I let everyone down because I have never done anything great or truly wonderful."

Within a few years Amazing succumbed to the belief that his life was a failure. To ease his inner suffering he turned to drink. He smoked. He gambled. He womanized. He sunk into a bottomless pit of self-pity and continued his loathsome ways for more than a half-century.

Finally, on his death bed, the final words he whispered to his wife were, "Whatever you do, don't put Amazing on my tombstone. It was bad enough to live with such a name. I don't want to carry it through eternity with me."

He was buried in the little cemetery on the hill above town. His wife purchased a large granite headstone inscribed with the words: *Here Lies Robert Jones, first white child born west of the Mississippi River.* But there was extra room and, on a whim, she decided to add: *Married 60 Years — Never Smoked — Never Gambled — Never Drank Spirits — Never Womanized.*

To this day people pause at the large granite headstone. They read the words and invariably they shake their heads and mutter, "Wow, that's amazing."

10

RATTLESNAKE LIES

Two old men were sitting around smoking hand-rolled cigarettes and swapping lies. The first one claimed, "I knew a fellow that was so tough that whenever he was bit by a rattlesnake it would never even make him sick and the snake would always die."

The other man said, "Well, I never knew anyone that tough but I did know a fellar who was out turning hay with a dump rake and something wasn't working quite right and he stopped to fix it. When he stepped down a rattlesnake commenced to rattle which spooked the horses and they ran off.

"The snake struck the fellar about midcalf and sunk his fangs in as far as they would go. It was quite a predicament and the fellar figured his only chance, and it was a slim one, was to try and walk to the ranch house.

"But after going less than a half-mile he began to feel light-headed and shortly after that the muscles in his leg cramped so bad he couldn't walk any more. He sat down on a log that was beside a little creek and figured himself a goner.

"Soon the big muscles in his back began to twitch and spasm. He was in a great deal of pain and told himself that if he was packing a gun he would end it. Then his hands and feet began to swell, swelled so bad he could not tell if he had fingers or toes. Then his eyes swelled shut and he lay down, said his prayers, and prepared himself to die.

"But he didn't die. In fact, when he woke up the swelling was gone. All around him the ground was littered two feet deep with the bodies of dead mosquitoes. They had saved his life by sucking out the snake venom."

11

BEE-LIEVE IT

Grandpa was a true gentleman in every sense of the word. As far as I know the taste of liquor never touched his lips nor did he ever smoke or engage in any behavior of a questionable nature. His only vice, if you want to call it a vice, was the fact he had a sweet tooth.

I have seen that man gobble down the entire contents of a box of chocolate-covered cherries without ever having the presence of mind to share with anyone else in the room. I watched him swipe fresh cookies off Grandma's cooling racks, one-by-one, when her back was turned, and he was not satisfied until he had devoured every last cookie in the batch. Grandma was so mad she wouldn't talk to him for a week.

Sometimes Grandpa was able to sooth his craving by searching out bee trees and robbing them of the honey. It takes patience to find a bee tree in the wild. First thing is to locate a spot where flowers are blooming and bees are working. In theory a bee, after it is loaded with nectar, will fly by the most direct route to the hive. Grandpa devised a trick. He dusted bees with flour and that made the tracking much easier.

One time Grandpa trailed bees to a big oak tree that was hollow on the inside. He squeezed through the narrow opening and feasted on honey. Afternoon turned to evening and when he did not return Grandma became worried and sent out the boys to look for Grandpa.

Eventually they found him and, believe it or not, the old man had eaten so much honey he was trapped and could not fit through the opening. The boys had to fetch an axe and chop him out or else he'd probably still be there.

MULES

The first storyteller rarely has a chance to tell the biggest yarn. Take the case of the oldtimers discussing the relative merits of mules.

The first man said, "Best mule I ever laid eyes on was a strawberry roan, name of Red. Belonged to a neighbor. When it came to pulling, wasn't a team nowhere could outpull Red. "Remember a time I was passing the neighbor's place and he was out plowing with Red. I listened ta him call out, 'Giddap, Doc. Come on, Jenny. Hup there, Blacky. Good job, Red....'

"When he completed the round I asked what he was doing, calling out like that, and he says, 'Well, I didn't want Red to think he was doing all the work by hisself.'

Another man chuckled. "Reminds me of Clyde. Back in those days had me a parcel of troublesome stumps. I hitched Clyde and tried to pull them free but had very little success. The only thing to do was to blow them with dynamite. But that took a lot of work because I had to dig down, place a charge, blow it and repeat the process several time before the roots would break loose.

"I worked all one morning and came in at noon, leaving the dynamite in the wagon. While I was eating Clyde ambled over to the wagon and stuck his nose into the case of dynamite.

"To make a long story short, when I came out of the house I saw Clyde where he didn't belong and hollered. This scared him. He jumped, came down on a rock, his shoes sparked, which in turn ignited the dynamite on his breath. The resulting explosion blew the wagon to smithereens, shoved the house 10 feet off its foundation and singed my beard. Clyde was sick to his stomach for dang near a week."

13

OL' BETSY

The old man spun his story the way a spider spins a web, with precision and painstaking patience.

"Most cherished possession is my rifle. Call her Ol' Betsy. Flintlock. Packs one heck of a wallop. Most accurate rifle in existence but slower than the second coming.

"To demonstrate what I'm talking about I'll tell this story about when I was living along the breaks of the Grand Canyon. Had me a cabin situated on a bench. One morning I step onto the porch and across the way, on the opposite side of the canyon, I spy a deer. If I squint I make out it's a buck with a sizable rack.

"I unlimbered Ol' Betsy, laid the barrel over the porch railing and took aim. Figuring the buck was so far away I would have to lob it in, I held the sight maybe twenty-feet high. I squeezed the trigger gentle as can be because at that distance every little mistake is amplified. Flint sparked, ignited the powder which set off the charge. Kaboom! The crashing sound echoed back and forth off the canyon walls, each boom growing fainter and more distant.

"When the smoke finally cleared I took a peek and way over there my buck was grazing like nothing out of the ordinary had happened. That definitely surprised me and, like I said, I had a powerful hunger for venison, so I took Ol' Betsy and commenced walking. I dropped down in the canyon and came up on the other side, sneaking into position. I was about ready to shoot when I heared a slow whistling sound followed by a dull thud. The buck dropped dead.

"Turned out Ol' Betsy was accurate but so slow that the bullet had just got there."

14

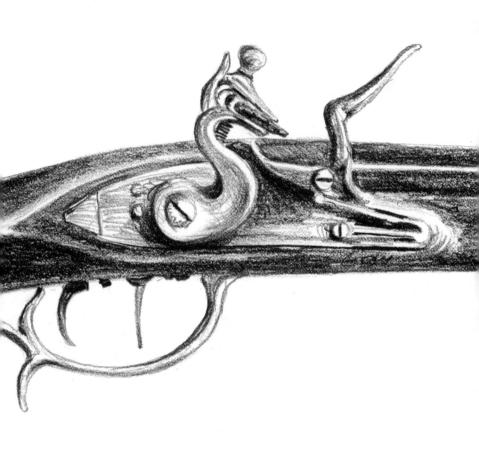

THE FREE DRINK

The buckaroo rode into town and dismounted. A tenderfoot approached, offered his hand and asked, "Are you a real cowboy?"

The buckaroo ignored the tenderfoot's hand and ambled in the direction of the nearest saloon. The tenderfoot tagged along and kept up a steady discourse about how he had just come west and how he had been looking forward to meeting a real cowboy. As they neared the front door of the saloon he asked, "May I buy you a drink?"

The buckaroo responded cordially, "Sure."

After buying several drinks the tenderfoot asked, "You never told me — are you a real cowboy?"

"Naw," said the buckaroo. "I don't work. Wish I could. I've got calves to brand, bulls to castrate, barren cows to cull. My old man is sick and weak. My brothers are worthless. And me, I can't do hardly nothin' at all...."

"Gee, you look strong and healthy," said the tenderfoot.

The buckaroo bragged, "I'm the strongest man in a hundred miles."

"If you are the strongest man in a hundred miles why can't you work?"

"Because," drawled the cowboy, "work is exercise and every time I exercise, my muscles develop so fast they split through my skin. Under my clothes I'm just a mass of scars."

With that said the buckaroo tossed down his drink, walked outside, remounted and rode away. All the tenderfoot could do was stare.

16

THE GOOSE HUNT

An old hermit lived far back in the woods by a small lake. One unusually long and cold winter he ran low on food. Not until the third week of March did the weather break and a spot near shore opened on the ice. The morning quiet was broken by the anxious chatter of a flock of geese. They dropped from the gray sky onto that small patch of water. The hermit was anxious to have fresh meat. He took his rifle off the pegs on the wall and sneaked toward the noise, being very deliberate in his approach. Slipping from tree to tree he could hear the geese splashing in the water and talking among themselves about how lucky they had been to find this open pool.

Finally the hermit reached a windfall, the last bit of cover between himself and the geese. He eased up and looked over. The geese had moved out of the water and were walking around on the ice. He waited for the opportune moment to kill the most geese with a single shot.

At last it came. The entire flock stepped to the edge of the open water for a drink. In unison they lowered their heads and then tilted them back. They were in a perfect line. The hermit took a deep breath, held it and squeezed the trigger. In a mad beating of wings and excited calls the geese rose into the sky and flew away.

The hermit could not believe his eyes. He ventured forth to investigate and discovered he had come as close to a feast as was possible. For years after the hermit would tell the story of the long winter and his goose hunt. And for evidence of how close he had come to bagging the entire flock, he would bring out a Mason jar with 17 goose beaks.

17

WALKAWAY

The kid from Missouri, having read every book Zane Grey wrote, decided to come west and live the adventurous life of a woodsman. His first day on the job he was setting chokers for a horse logger who went by the name Walkaway.

"Walkaway, now that's a mighty unusual name. How in the world did you come by such a name?" inquired the kid.

Walkaway gave the kid a hard look. "Hold these," he muttered and handed him the lines to the team. He turned, ambled off and disappeared into the brush.

After a few moments of inactivity one of the horses pawed the ground while the other shivered dust off her back. The kid said, "Take it easy. Work's always gonna be here. Be patient, gals."

For a while the woods were absolutely quiet and then the kid noticed birds flitting around the tops of the trees singing happy melodies. The team counted time by swishing their long tails at persistent horseflies. Finally, to break the monotony, the kid began whistling. The horses perked their ears but the birds paid no mind.

It was well past lunch when the bull boss happened to come along. "Why are you holdin' the team? And where is Walkaway?"

"Don't rightly know," said the kid with a shrug. "All I know is I was trying to make conversation and he up and handed me the lines, said to hold 'em."

"What'd ya say?" the bull buck wanted to know.

"Just asked how he came by his name," replied the kid.

"Oh no," moaned the bull buck. "He's a might touchy about personal matters. Guess he's done walked away, again."

GIANT MOSQUITOES

"Modern mosquitoes are a nuisance but when I first came into this country the mosquitoes were deadly," told the pioneer. "The first night I arrived I camped down along the river. The moon came up and all of a sudden I heard this noise. I glanced skyward and to my shock and utter amazement I saw this squadron of giant mosquitoes flying across the moon, coming straight toward my camp.

"The team heard them and spooked, pulled loose from where I had them staked and went running over the hill. I had no choice but to stand my ground and fight. I armed myself with a heavy maul and took cover inside an iron boiler in the wagon. I huddled there listening to the loud droning of the mosquitoes as they reconnoitered, calculating, I suppose, their plan of assault.

"The attack was swift and sure. They came at the boiler from all sides, battering it with their bodies. But the boiler was made from heavy iron and it did not give, or even dent. And then one of the terrible insects reared back and drove his stinger into the metal. It poked inside and nearly struck me. Reacting with speed and veracity I used my maul to bend over the stinger. More stingers appeared and these I used the maul on, too.

"The pitch of the buzzing changed. The mosquitoes, mad at being trapped, beat their wings furiously and I could feel the wagon shake and then begin to actually lift off the ground.

At that point I realized the mosquitoes were going to carry the wagon, and me, away. Squirming my way from under the boiler and taking a moment to locate my muzzle-loading shotgun, I blasted away until every last one of the giant mosquitos were dead."

19

FIFTY-YEAR FISH

Two men had gone out together on the opening day of fishing season, to the same fishing hole, for the past 49 years. But as the 50th year approached they had a disagreement. The first man said, "I want to go back to that same spot. We've always caught fish there."

The second man said, "I was thinking about trying somewhere new."

And so, for the first time in a half century, they agreed to go their separate ways. They met the following Monday. The first man asked his friend, "Well, how did you do? That new spot pay off?"

"Most certainly did," beamed the second man. "I got there just as the dawn was breaking, baited up with a big ol' juicy worm and cast out. Then I waited. The sun came up and I figured that as the day warmed the fish would start biting. Along about mid-morning my bobber started acting funny, twitching a little. I grabbed up my rod and waited. Sure enough the bobber disappeared and I set the hook.

"Did I ever have a dandy! Thought I had hooked onto a freight train. That's what it felt like. We battled back and forth for most of an hour before I was able to land it."

"What did he weigh?" asked the first man.

"Rainbow trout — 32 pounds. So, how did you do?"

"Had me a bunch of nibbles, finally got a good strike. We tussled back and forth and I managed to reel him in. Would you believe that he had wrapped himself around the handle of the lantern, that one you lost back in 1937? The crazy part was the light was still on."

The second man looked a little sheepish. "All right, I'll knock 30 pounds off my fish if you change your story and at least turn the light off."

PARACHUTE AND THE CHOKER

This story has been told in logging camps from Colorado to British Columbia. It goes like this:

An old lady and a logger were riding in an airplane. All of a sudden the engine sputtered. "What's wrong?" the logger asked.

The pilot replied, "Nothing to worry about."

Then the engine quit altogether and the nose of the airplane dropped. The pilot turned to his passengers and yelled, "I've got some bad news. I only have one parachute."

He held up the parachute. And then he grabbed at his chest and died from a massive heart attack. The parachute fell between the old woman and the logger.

"You take it," the logger said.

"Oh no," said the woman. "You take it. You must have a family. How many children do you have?"

"Five, three boys and two girls, ranging in age from 19 all the way down to six months," replied the logger.

"That settles it," said the old woman. "My husband passed away last year. We never had children. I have no one to live for. You take the parachute."

"Can't," the logger told her as he twisted around and began pawing through suitcases and boxes.

"Please," the old woman insisted, "for the sake of your family, take the parachute and jump before it's too late."

The logger pulled loose a braided wire cable. "This is what I was after. This choker. I've been setting these for twenty years. They fasten around logs so they can be hauled to the landing. I've set thousands.

"You take the parachute. I'll jump with this. Based on my years of experience I can absolutely guarantee, somewhere between here and the ground, this choker is gonna hang up on somethin'."

21

A QUESTION OF WEATHER

A traveler entered the mercantile store where a half-dozen men were gathered around a potbelly stove. Trying to make conversation he inquired, "So, what do you fellows think the weather is going to do?"

"Only a dang fool or a newcomer would try to predict the weather," groused one man.

"Weather!" exclaimed another man, "I tell you it rained 18 inches at my place last evening. On this side of the mountains we measure rain a little different though, here we measure the number of inches between drops."

A third man entered the conversation. "'Round this neck of the woods it's generally so dry you have ta be primed 'fore you can spit."

A fourth offered, "One time the neighbor hand-dug himself a well. He hoarded that water like it was gold, he did. One day a twister came along and sucked every bit of water out of that well. The air was so dry that it vaporized, all except one drop which fell and hit his daughter on her forehead. Surprised her so much she fainted and it took two buckets of sand to bring her around."

"Sounds 'bout right," said the fifth man. "Dry as a bone around these parts and the wind, Lordy, does the wind blow! One time I was coming past a sodbuster's house and he was fixing a weather contraption, hanging a logging chain from a tall pole. When I asked how it worked he said that when the chain was hanging straight out it was a gentle breeze. But when the links started snapping off the end, then it was classified as a real wind.

"That's nothing," claimed the sixth man. "I remember the time I was digging fence holes in Colorado and the wind came up, blew so hard that I had to travel all the way to Nevada before I found where they landed."

With that the traveler, shaking his head, departed.

STOP AND LIE

Harold Lemons was a washed-up old cowboy known far and wide as a teller of tall tales. The following story demonstrates his remarkable gift.

One time Harold was driving a buckboard along the road when a couple of men on horseback overtook him. As they drew near one called, "Hey, Harold, pull up. Shoot the breeze with us. Tell us a lie."

Harold kept his team headed down the road. "Sorry, boys. Ain't got time to stop and tell a lie. Not today."

"How come not?"

"Because an old timer around these parts passed on," said Harold. He removed the bandanna from around his neck and wiped his face. "I'm headed to town to buy lumber. I'm gonna make a coffin and bury one of the best friends a man could ever have."

"If he's already dead, it ain't agonna matter. Take a minute, stop, tell us a lie. We need the entertainment."

Harold was resolute. "Not today, boys."

"Who was it that died?"

"Old man Flanary," said Harold with a sad shake of his head.

"I'll be darned," said one of the men. "Didn't even know he was sick."

"Wasn't," claimed Harold. "Come on sudden like."

"Sorry to hear that." Spurs flashed and the two horses moved along at a faster pace. "See you later."

The Flanary place was only a mile or so from town and as the two men drew near they spotted old man Flanary, very much alive, sitting on his front porch, rocking back and forth, playing his fiddle.

It took a minute to sink in. Harold was such an accomplished liar he did not have to stop and tell a lie, he could tell a lie and keep right on going.

WINDY

Out west farmers are prone to extol the deep, black humus soil in the river bottoms brought in by centuries of floods. One farmer offered the following tall testimony.

"I remember the time a neighbor accidentally dropped a corn kernel near his back porch. Within a few hours a corn stalk had grown above the eaves of the cabin. The next morning his boy started climbing the stalk and in no time flat he was way up in the air. The stalk was growing amazingly fast. The youngster kept getting farther and farther away and began hollering, 'Dad! Help me!'

"His father rushed to the back porch and went to work on the corn stalk with an axe. But every gash he made would be way over his head by the time he swung again. Instead of saving his son, the father had to stand there and listen to the pitiful cries recede into the sky.

"Undoubtedly the boy lived some time existing on corn, because cobs kept landing near the base. The father was so grieved by this that his heart gave out and he died. When he reached heaven he asked Saint Peter, 'Where is my son?'

"'I don't believe he is here,' replied Saint Peter.

"'You're mistaken,' interjected the father. 'He was always a good boy. Never did anything wrong. But several weeks ago he started climbing a corn stalk and it was growing so fast he disappeared above the clouds and that was the last I've seen of him.'

"'Oh, that boy!' drawled Saint Peter. 'Of course. He came through here but he was going so fast we couldn't stop him.'

"That's my story and it points out just how dang good the soil is 'round these parts on the creek bottom."

THE WIDOW'S COW

A widow lived on a hill beside the railroad tracks. One evening her milk cow wandered onto the tracks and was hit and killed by a locomotive.

The following morning the widow visited the railroad office and insisted they pay, telling the official, "I was here long before the railroad. You owe me for my cow."

But the railroad man said, "We don't see it that way. Maybe you will learn a lesson from this and keep your stock off our right-of-way."

"You're gonna be sorry," the widow warned. At home she cut fat from the dead cow and made soft soap, which she poured onto the rails on the grade. The next train to come to the hill spun its drive wheels until the locomotive came to a shuddering stop and began to slowly slide backwards. The train slid all the way to the bottom and the engineer and conductor, grumbling and cursing, went about the task of shoveling dirt onto the rails for traction.

That night the widow washed the rails and applied another liberal layer of soap. This continued for a week and then the railroad attorney paid the widow a visit.

"We know what you are doing. When we catch you in the act we will prosecute you to the full extent of the law."

In a firm voice the widow replied, "I am a patient woman. I can wait as long as necessary. I shall use every opportunity to my advantage. You will never catch me."

The attorney removed his hat, wiped at his brow with a kerchief and asked, "How much do you figure your cow was worth?"

The widow told him a fair price. The attorney replaced his hat. "I suppose that in the long run it would be far cheaper to pay you than contend with your sabotaging the railroad. I shall meet your demand."

THE DROUGHT

Grandpa was a very resourceful man and when the terrible drought struck, the neighbors paid Grandpa a visit, asking his assistance to help bring rain.

For a long time Grandpa sat contemplating possibilities. All at once he smiled broadly and said, "I want you all to go home and prepare a picnic lunch, then spread a blanket on the ground under a shade tree, sit down and have a nice, happy meal."

While the neighbors were busy Grandpa sneaked off to the dried-up spring. Presently he found what he was looking for and triumphantly held up a skinny frog. He pulled his pocket watch from his vest and began swinging it back and forth while repeating over and over in a monotonous tone, "You are growing very sleepy, very, very sleepy."

Presently the frog's eyelids grew heavy and he closed his eyes, hypnotized. Then Grandpa told the frog, "A big storm is rolling in from out of the north. The clouds are black with moisture and the sky begins to drip. A few raindrops hit. The dry ground drinks them up. The rain comes harder, faster. The ground guzzles its fill. Puddles form here and there. Can you feel the rain, feel the way the fat, cool drops collide against your dry skin? Isn't the rain wonderful? Don't you want to sing?"

The frog lifted his lone voice and let forth a loud croak that echoed off the hillsides. All the other frogs heard this plaintive cry and were tricked into croaking. And the rain god heard the racket of a thousand frogs lifting their collective voices, looked down and saw all the people enjoying picnic lunches and knew that it was time. He filled his lungs and blew in a terrific storm.

And that is the true story of how Grandpa ended the drought.

ROANY

The outdoorsman sat on his haunches watching the campfire send a shower of lively sparks into the inky black sky. After a moment he began his story.

"It was a night like this, blacker than a pile of Angus cows. So black, in fact, all the bats stayed home.

"That night I was making my way into Snake River canyon leading a pack string and riding Roany. Roany was my all-time favorite horse, a dark red roan, handsome, dependable and sure-footed as a billy goat on a rock pile.

"All of a sudden, real abrupt-like, Roany comes to a stop. "I say, 'Come on, boy. What's got into you?'

"He snorts. I ask him, 'Do you smell a cougar? Bear? Bet it's a she bear and she probably has cubs.'

"Roany shakes his head side to side, tells me it ain't a cougar, ain't a bear. I kick him in the ribs with my heels and tell him, 'If it ain't nothing at all let's get a move on. I don't wanna wait here all night.'

"I kick Roany in the ribs, beg him, get mad and yell. Roany does not move. Not so much as even a flinch.

"In disgust I hop off. I am gonna lead him but when I get in front of him my feet go out from under me real sudden-like. I've stepped off a cliff. I have a death-grip on the reins and the force of the fall causes me to pull Roany after me.

"We're falling fast, air just a'whistling in my ears. All of a sudden it comes to me what I have to do. I holler out, 'Whoa! Whoa there, Roany! Whoa!'

"He sets his feet in mid-air, pulls back with all his might and somehow I manage to hang on. Turns out when Roany finally comes to a stop the pointed tips of my cowboy boots are just barely touchin' solid ground."

NIMBLE

The pot and pan salesman arrived at the desert camp just as the sun was tumbling from the sky. He stopped his mule team and inquired of the buckaroos gathered around a small fire, "Would you gentlemen be offended if I spent the night with you?"

One of the men took a noisy sip of coffee from a tin mug before he replied, "Suit yerself."

The salesman tended his mules and then joined the group. Someone handed him a cup of steaming, black coffee and while he waited for it to cool he kept up a steady banter. The buckaroos responded to any question directed their way with a simple, "Yep," "Nope," or "Don't rightly know."

Eventually the salesman ran low on conversation and happened to ask, "So, any of you gentlemen ever owned a mule?"

This question brought one buckaroo to life. He stood and answered exuberantly, "Yes, I have and a mighty nimble mule he was. Let me tell you...."

The man built a smoke, lit it with a twig from the fire and finally continued. "Time comes to mind was the night I was riding through High Pass. No moon, no stars. But I wasn't worried. That mule was mighty nimble on his feet.

"All of a sudden it gives a snort like it smelt a cougar. Goes three ways from Sunday. And like a greased horseshoe slidin' down an iron chute he does a backward flip with a quick spin, lands on its feet an' is headed back down the trail goin' the opposite direction."

A long moment passed and then the salesman tests the validity of the story by questioning, "When he flipped over like that did he buck you off?"

"Naw," replied the buckaroo taking a long drag off his cigarette, blowing out a cloud of smoke. "But I did get the top of my Stetson hat a tad dusty."

30

STINK BUG

Uncle Ben was known as a frequent imbiber. In fact, he brewed his own personal blend of spirituous liquor and carried a small flask in his hind pocket at all times. He claimed he saved it only for special occasions.

One such special occasion took place on a fishing trip when he forgot to bring along the can of worms. He searched high and low, turning over logs and rocks looking for some likely insect that he could substitute for bait; but there was nothing to find until he spied a big stink bug in a clump of crested wheat grass.

He picked it up and, thinking he should freshen it a bit, removed his flask and poured a healthy shot down the open mouth of the black bug. He worked the bug onto the hook and threw his bait into the lake.

For a time the bobber sat on the flat sheen of the water and then it began doing funny things. It dipped and danced and finally plunged under the surface.

Uncle Ben grabbed up the rod and a terrific battle ensued. Line was pulled off at a furious rate. The reel began smoking so badly that Uncle Ben, fearing it would burn up, dipped it in the water to cool it. When there were only a few more yards of line left on the reel he hurriedly tied off to a nearby tree.

For the next couple of hours he pulled in line hand over hand, finally managing to yard the fish up on the bank. It was a bass, the granddaddy of all bass.

What confounded my Uncle Ben was the fact that the fish did not have the hook in his mouth. It turned out the stink bug had wrapped its arms and legs around the bass's lip and it could not be coaxed into letting go until a liberal dose of spirits was poured into its open mouth.

31

REBEL

A woodsman told this whopper. "I grew up in the back country, the bush we called it. For something to do I ran a trap line and every day after school I checked my traps. Did that for five or six winters.

"There was a fellow, lived a few miles from us, who died unexpectedly and we took in his dog named Rebel. He walked me to school, stayed through the day and went with me in the late afternoons to check my traps.

"Strictly by accident I discovered Rebel possessed a remarkable talent. The revelation became evident the time I leaned a muskrat drying board against the woodshed. The next morning I went to bring in an armload of wood and there was a dead muskrat lying beside the drying board. I patted Rebel's head and told him what a fine dog he was.

"To test him I lay one of my coyote drying boards against the woodshed. The following morning I discovered a freshly-killed coyote lying beside it.

"During the course of the next several weeks Rebel brought in beaver, raccoon, muskrat, skunks and coyotes. One morning I went outside and Rebel was nowhere to be found. I called and called. Went down to the creek but there was no sign Rebel had been there.

"I looked up the road and finally saw Rebel dragging a raccoon skin coat, chased by college-aged boys driving a Model-A. Not until later was I able to piece together what had transpired. Ma, needing Papa to do some work on her ironing board, had leaned it against the woodshed.

"Papa gave the coat back to the boys and Rebel never hunted again. Guess he figured it wasn't worth him going to all the effort if we were gonna give the hide back to the critter."

KID AND THE KITE

When I was a kid we lived miles from any neighbor and as a result I learned how to entertain myself. One of my favorite pastimes was flying a kite.

One year I built a huge kite, so big I was forced to use a stout rope instead of a string. I tied one end to our buckboard, launched the kite and stood watching as it climbed into the air. But the knot wasn't very good and it started to come loose. I ran to the buckboard and grabbed the end of the rope just as it came untied.

The next thing I knew, the force of the rising kite had jerked me off my feet and up into the air. I was too high to consider dropping. All I could do was hold on and pray. I flew higher and higher. The air became very cold and the wind more powerful. I had to do something but was temporarily paralyzed by fear. Luckily I have a fertile imagination and a bright idea came to me.

I always carried a slingshot tucked into my belt and my trouser pockets full of small rocks, just in case I came upon a ground squirrel or a jackrabbit. Needless to say I was a crack shot. I wrapped the rope securely around my waist, pulled my slingshot free and loaded the pouch with a small pebble. I took aim at the kite and fired, punching a hole in one side. The kite fluttered and quickly I put another hole in the opposite side so as to keep the kite on an even keel.

I kept punching holes in the kite until it quit climbing. Once we started down the wind was weaker and I began losing altitude at an alarming rate. Always a quick thinker I removed my shirt and threw it against the kite. But the kite was so big and I had shot so many holes in it that I had to remove my trousers and throw those, too.

Eventually I landed. Then I had a long walk home and some tall explaining to my mother when I got there.

IN NEED OF A DRINK

"I used to be a bit of a drinker," claimed the old man. "And the story I am fixing to relate occurred during the pro-hi days. "Know anything about prohibition? It began in 19 'n' 19 when the federal government outlawed alcohol. Proved to be an unpopular law and bootlegging, the illegal making and distribution of alcoholic beverages, became a moneymaking operation until the law was finally repealed in '33.

"During prohibition the only place a person could legally purchase alcohol was at a drug store. One time I was traveling through a small town and for the life of me I could not discover any bootleggers in the vicinity who could be called upon to satisfy my craving.

"At long last I went to the local drug store and asked for a bottle of medicinal whiskey.

"'Can't sell you any,' claimed the druggist.

"'But I'm sick,' I lied.

"'Sick from what?' he wanted to know.

"'Digestion's gone bad. Can't sleep. Nerves on edge. If I just had a nip of whiskey I'd be fine,' I lied again.

"He shook his head, 'According to the law, none of the ailments you quoted allow me to sell you alcohol.'

"I was desperate. 'Well, what ailment would allow you to sell me a bottle?' I asked him.

"'The sheriff in these parts allows me to dispense whiskey only in the case of a rattlesnake bite,' he replied.

"I was trying to understand. 'If I was to tell you I had been bitten by a rattlesnake then you would be obliged to sell me a bottle of whiskey?'

"'No sir,' he said. 'I could not sell you a bottle because we have one rattlesnake in this town and his services have already been booked for the next three weeks.'"

SPECIAL CHICKENS

Some men were born with a special skill to work with their hands and some were born to work with their heads. Precious few were born to work with both and the most famous of this breed was a blacksmith named Samuel Parker.

He came west early, parked his wagon along the route of the Oregon Trail and was there to do iron work and shoeing when the pioneers came through. Later, when the pioneers became farmers, Parker was called on to fashion special parts. And later still, when the automobile came into existence, Parker changed his blacksmith shop to a garage and kept right on earning a living.

Parker is the rightful inventor of most of the modern-day inventions. Who do you think taught the basic skills of inventing to such recognized men as Alexander Graham Bell, Thomas Edison and Eli Whitney? It was just that Parker never sought publicity. He would much rather be working in his shop than making headlines in the newspaper.

The fact of the matter is that Parker was so talented with his thinking and his hands that he even invented a special breed of fowl. It came about the year of the big flood. There was so much water and it stayed wet so long that all through the country chickens were dying from starvation because their feet were sinking in the mud and they could not forage.

It was a desperate situation but as usual Parker invented a solution. He fired up his forge and made webbing that fit between the chickens' toes and, carrying matters a step further, he heated up the chickens' pointed beaks and flattened them with a hammer so they would be better adapted to probing underwater for insects and grass shoots.

The birds took to the water and actually learned to swim. A group of local Indians were watching these birds feed and they came up with a name for what eventually became an entirely new species — they called them ducks.

GIANT HOPPERS

During the summer of '33 the grasshoppers were so thick that clouds of them blocked out the sun and chickens would go to the roost thinking night had fallen. They wiped out that year's crops.

The following spring one farmer hit upon the idea of importing wild turkeys. His assumption was that wild turkeys would eat their weight in hoppers every day and that would stem the infestation. As an added benefit he and his neighbors would have fat turkeys to dine on come Thanksgiving.

The farmer sent off for fertile eggs and when they arrived he enlisted a small army of banty hens to set on them. Three weeks later the turkeys hatched and the farmer took great care in giving them a healthy start in life. Before long they were running around catching baby hoppers.

But while the turkeys were growing the hoppers were growing even faster. In fact, the hoppers became so big and aggressive that they began to terrorize the turkeys, spitting juice at them and even attacking when one wandered too far from the flock. When that happened the embarrassed turkey would return to the farm completely nude because the hoppers had plucked and eaten every feather.

The huge hoppers soon began chasing the turkeys. The turkeys were terrified. They flew until they grew tired and then they ran. All the while the giant hoppers drove them forward with slashing kicks from their powerful hind legs.

The turkeys did not have time to stop and eat and gradually began to lose weight and shrink in size. Few people today realize that the descendants of the original wild turkeys imported during the great hopper invasion of the 1930s is the game bird we call quail.

THE WILDS

One of the amusements of the Western cowboy was stringing along a tenderfoot. A common topic of conversation at a tenderfoot's first evening in camp was rattlesnakes — how they were cold-blooded and oftentimes crawled in a man's bedroll during the night.

"If you wake up and discover a snake beside you, lie real still. Don't move so much as a muscle. Do and you're dead."

"Maybe I'll just sleep in the chuckwagon," was a common response.

With great solemnness another cowboy stated, "Don't much matter. Out here snakes climb as well as they slither. They can be up a wagon wheel and into a box as fast as a skinny lizard scootin' over a hot rock in the noonday sun."

While the tenderfoot tried to digest this latest information the cowboys sipped coffee. Out in the dark a hungry coyote let forth a string of sharp yips and the tenderfoot, hackles raised, stuttered, "W-W-What's t-t-that?"

A cowboy declared, "Only one thing it can be. Beargar. That's a cross 'tween a bear an' a cougar. Strong as a bear, swift as a cougar. One of 'em get's a whiff of human scent an'...."

"Maybe it'll stay upwind," offered the tenderfoot.

The cowboy shook his head, muttered, "Naw, he'll circle an' most likely, 'fore mornin', one of us'll be gone." That said, the cowboys tossed out the remaining coffee in their cups, unrolled their bedrolls and promptly went to sleep on the ground.

The tenderfoot sat up all night, keeping the fire going while listening to the snoring of the men and the noises of the nocturnal creatures. The next morning he headed back to the city, bent on never spending another night in the wilds.

DRAW

A real bragger can, by twirling a few well-chosen words, take something insignificant and make that trivial thing into a work of art. Consider the old woodsman describing the draw of a fireplace.

"My old man could make a fireplace and, boy-oh-boy, would she ever draw! The best one he ever built was when we were living in the woods. We put together a dandy log cabin, big fir logs and a porch that ran the entire length. Along a side wall we built a fireplace out of river rock, used a slab of cedar for the mantle and was it ever a pretty red color.

"I was just a kid at the time, 10 or 11 years old, but I recall it like yesterday — Dad laying out a fire with some pitch and dry kindling, lighting it. He told me to go fetch some wood.

"At that time we had a Redbone hound and she was about to have puppies. She was tied to a post on the front porch. When I opened the front door to get the wood for the fire the draft created from the fireplace set up a whirlwind like you could not believe. I was out of the main part of the wind but that poor hound dog wasn't so fortunate. She was pulled toward the door, far as the chain would allow, and four pups were pulled out of her before Dad could scatter the fire.

"The best part of that fireplace was that any time the fire started to die down all we had to do was open the front door and the draw would suck chunks of fresh wood straight off the woodpile.

"Now that's a mighty fine draw."

DREAM

It was Halloween and the grandkids wanted Grandfather to tell them a scary story. He obliged.

"This tale happened the time I got caught out miles away from civilization and was forced to spend the night at a line shack. There were stories that the place was haunted on account of gold buried around there.

"I threw my bedroll on the floor and was soon asleep. All of a sudden the door blew open and banged against the wall with a loud thud. I opened my eyes. A crescent moon was shining, giving off enough light that I could see a woman holding a shovel. She was dressed in a long white gown. She pointed a long finger at me, beckoned me. I did as she commanded.

"She handed me the shovel. I took it. When I looked up she was floating through the tall grasses. Again she beckoned and I followed to an enormous tree where spreading branches blocked out all but a faint glow from the moon. She pointed down and I understood that she wanted me to dig in that particular spot.

"The ground was soft. A couple feet down my shovel hit something. I scrambled to my hands and knees, felt around and found the gaping mouth of a three-pound coffee can. There was something inside.

"That's when I woke up. I don't know what was in there. All I know is that I had shoved my hand in my mouth and I was holding this." With that Grandfather displayed his set of false teeth, making them snap together.

QUAIL HUNT

The locals were gathered around the potbelly stove in the general store drinking coffee and swapping yarns about the way things used to be in the old days. The front door opened and swept inside with a gust of Arctic air was a city hunter.

The proprietor asked, "What can I do for you, mister?"

"A box of shotgun shells," requested the hunter.

"What gauge, what size shot?" asked the store owner.

"Twelve gauge. I'm going after quail," replied the hunter.

"You need game loads, seven-and-a-half probably do you best," he was told.

One of the men who was warming his backside muttered to the other oldtimers, "If he expects to put any meat on the table he better get three or four boxes of shells. Those quail are hard to hit...." He went on to tell a long involved story that demonstrated how difficult quail were to hunt for even a skilled woodsman and a crack shot such as himself.

As the out-of-towner was paying for the shells he asked the storekeeper, "Where would be a good place to hunt?"

The proprietor called to the locals, "Where would you suggest this gentleman try hunting quail?"

"The old Taylor place," came the answer.

The proprietor gave directions and concluded by saying, "Check the haystack. There are always a couple of coveys hanging around there."

An hour later the hunter returned. One of the men called, "Well, how did you do?"

"Real good," claimed the man. "I got 14."

"What did you do, ground sluice them before they could fly?"

"You mean they can fly?" replied the hunter in surprise.

BIRD DOG

Most bird hunters like to brag about their hunting dogs, often to the point of stretching the truth. So it was with old Lefty and his bird dog, Babe.

"Babe was the finest dog ever put down on God's green earth. She's gone now but to demonstrate what I mean, I'll tell about the time she and I were hunting quail.

"Babe picks up fresh scent, nose goes to the ground and she stays on the trail over rock slides and through sagebrush thick as bristles on a hog's back. With her tail wagging she disappears over this little ridge.

"I follow along, going real slow, real cautious and careful like 'cause I know that at any instant there's gonna be quail going three ways from Sunday.

"From on the other side of the rise I hear the whir of wings and presently a single quail rises above the skyline. Up goes my shotgun. I fire. The quail tumbles. A second bird flashes and I get him. And then a third, fourth, fifth.

"This is real peculiar because quail never come out single file. Usually the whole covey explodes at once, birds everywhere and you never know which one to take and get all confused and more than likely you get nothing at all except blue sky and embarrassment.

"Anyways, I call Babe but nothing happens. That is going too far because Babe always comes when I call. Birds six, seven and eight come up like ducks in a shooting gallery.

"By now I am curious as all get out. I drop to my hands and knees, ease up and peek over the ridge top.

"And there is Babe. She has rounded up a covey, forced them into a rabbit hole. Her front paws are over the entrance and she's allowing only one quail at a time to escape.

"Yep, that was Babe. Never been a dog before or since like her."

THE AXE MAN'S TEST

Back in the boom days of logging, a new man to the woods was required to undergo an initiation. One way to find out what a newcomer was made of was to administer the axe man's test.

Usually at lunch break or after the day's work was completed a logger would approach the greenhorn and ask, "Ever take the axe man's test?"

"No, I haven't," would be the reply.

The crew would gather, a chopping block would be produced and directions would be given. "All you have to do is use your axe and hit the same spot on the block four times in a row. Can you do it?"

"I think so."

"The catch is you have to do it with your eyes closed. And you have to keep them closed between swings. Still want to give it a try?"

The greenhorn, wanting to make a good impression, would agree. Lifting his axe over his head, eyes closed, he would swing the ax once, twice, three times.

Then one of the loggers would grab the new man's gloves, or lunch bucket, whatever was handy, and place it on the chopping block. The final swing would come smashing down followed by a wild chorus of laughter.

For the next few weeks the new man would be teased about the incident. If he took the ribbing good-naturedly and if he did his share of the work then, in time, he would be welcomed into the fraternity of loggers.

THE DRINK AND THE SHOVEL

Call it moonshine, snake poison, rot gut, coffin varnish, wild mare juice.... By any name the consumption of alcohol can turn a normal man into an absolute fool.

A perfect example of this occurred one time when a fellow from over on the flats drank too much in town. On the way home he came to a jog in the road where a farmer was shoveling grain into a high-sided wagon. The field was located on a mesa that dropped off to a meandering river. The fellow stopped and, with slurred speech, commented that a swim would feel dandy. He asked the farmer the easiest way to get to the river.

"Next farm down, old Adkin place, go through the barnyard, can't miss the trail," said the farmer.

The drinking man peered over the edge of the mesa and, noticing a gravel slide that ran all the way to the river's edge, a reckless idea occurred to him. He offered, "Give you five bucks for that scoop shovel."

"Sold," said the farmer.

The fellow took another swig from the bottle to boost his confidence and then, plopping unceremoniously onto the large scoop shovel, he pushed off and started down the long gravel chute. He had positioned the handle between his legs thinking it would allow him the ability to steer.

Hurtling downhill, friction between the metal and the gravel quickly caused the shovel to glow red-hot. Near the bottom of the slide there was a terrible wreck. Dust boiled. All of a sudden the man, with his pants down around his ankles, shot from the dust cloud and stumbled down the bank and into the river where he sat for an exceedingly long time.

It was said that the man took his meals in a standing position for some time and that forever after he gave up the drinking of intoxicating spirits.

UNTIL IT RAINS

What began as a few days of sunshine stretched into weeks of absolutely perfect weather. After a while folks began to worry about what they referred to as "the drought".

Across backyard fences people said, "Lordy, Lordy, what a scorcher. If only it would cloud up and rain."

At sunup and sundown farmers nervously searched the horizon for any small cloud and at night they watched for signs of a ring around the moon. But there was no end to the drought as day after day continued like perfect beads strung on an endless necklace.

"Our grain is gonna shrivel up ta nothin'," claimed one farmer. "And if we don't get a harvest the bank will foreclose. If there aren't farmers, there's no sense having a town. We gotta have rain. That's all there is to it."

"What can we do?" asked the farm implement dealer.

"Maybe something," said the editor of the local newspaper. "I've heard stories that in the old days Indian medicine men would perform a rain dance. We ought to get an Indian to give us a rain dance."

A spokesman from the nearby reservation was contacted and arrangements were made for the tribal medicine man to dance. For a substantial fee he guaranteed rain.

The newspaper editor interviewed the Indian and wanted to know, "How often have you actually made it rain?"

"One hundred percent of the time."

"That's remarkable," said the editor. "What a tremendous record. How long will you dance?"

The medicine man, in a stoic voice, replied, "Until it rains."

FARMER'S TALE

"Scratching a living from the ground, even in the best of times, is an iffy situation," claimed the farmer.

"I remember one year we got all sorts of rain, so much that I was beginning to worry that it would interfere or maybe even ruin the corn harvest. Water came up fast. I was scared to death it was going to drown the field. But it turned out that was the least of my worries 'cause the carp came over the levy and invaded the fields. Those blasted carp were the hungriest critters on God's green earth. They could eat a fellow out of house and home in no time flat.

"It just so happened I had me a pretty fair pony and I took to riding him between rows and roping carp with a lasso. It was sort of a trick 'cause I couldn't get a full swing but anyways I've always been more or less of a hand with a rope. Once the loop went over their heads I had to pull up the slack real quick-like or those fish would wiggle free. Once I had hold of a carp I would take a dally around the saddle horn and let my horse play him until the fish was fairly docile. Then I would hop down and finish the job with a sledge hammer delivered to the fish's noggin.

"It wasn't long before the fish got wise. They would only come out at night. I didn't know how they were seeing until I stayed up and watched. To my utter and complete surprise there were thousands upon thousands of fireflies flitting around the tasseled stalks furnishing light to the fish.

"So I caught fireflies and dipped their tails in black paint. By the end of the week there wasn't any more light and by then the water had dropped. My corn crop was saved."

BISCUITS

Stormy Jordan was between jobs when he stumbled into George Stanford's logging camp. He asked if there was any work available and Stanford told him, "Not unless you can cook. The one I had just walked out on us."

Stormy was desperate for a job and lied, "Just so happens cooking is my specialty."

That evening when the crew returned from the woods Stormy called out, "Come an' get it!"

Big Charley Day, one of the fallers, reached toward the mound of biscuits on the plate. He lifted one, felt its weight, peered at it and shook his head. He dunked an edge of it in his coffee but it was too hard to bite and in disgust he hurled the offending biscuit against the wall.

Stormy chose that precise moment to reenter the room with a platter of food. The biscuit ricocheted off the wall and hit him in the back of the head. He stopped dead in his tracks. Quiet lasted for an exaggerated moment and then the room erupted in laughter.

Stormy's expression never changed. He carefully set the platter on the table, turned on his heels and exited the room. He went to the bunkhouse, secured his Colt revolver, returned to the mess hall and marched directly to Big Charley Day. He shoved the pistol forward until the round barrel was resting at a point midway between Charley's eyes. He growled, "I've already got one notch for killing a man. Another doesn't mean much."

He kept the pistol where it was but addressed the other men, "Try a biscuit. See what you think of my cooking."

Hands reached for the plate and teeth attempted to bite into the hard biscuits. Stormy's voice boomed, "What do you men have to say?"

In unison husky voices called out, "Not half bad." "Pretty dang good." "Tasty. Yep, mighty tasty."

FISH AND GROUSE

It used to be that a family lived according to how proficient the man of the house happened to be at hunting and fishing.

"My wife and kids never went hungry," one man bragged. "I remember this particularly productive fishing trip. It was customary for me to wear gumboots, the same ones I wore doing chores. I waded into the river and cast toward the deep hole where the big trout tended to congregate.

"No sooner had the bait hit the water than a fish gobbled it. I figured it was a good-sized fish and reared back to set the hook, but it turned out to be a small fish that went flying up and out of the water. My hook popped loose.

"The trout landed behind me in the bushes. It so happened that a grouse was sitting on a nest in there and she got scared with all the commotion and came out in a flurry of flapping wings and wild squawks. She flew within a whisker of my baited hook, struck at it and the hook lodged in her beak. She flew off but when she hit the end of the slack line the force upset my balance, I fell into the water and floundered around like a carp left out in the noonday sun. Somehow I managed to regain my senses and start reeling.

"That grouse fought better than any fish I ever caught. To make a long story short I won the battle and when the grouse was within reach I managed to grab her and wring her neck.

"After that I scrambled up the bank. There was something squirming around in my boots and when I checked I'll be darned if I didn't empty 11 fish out of my gumboots.

"Eleven plus the original one made an even dozen, added to a grouse and fourteen eggs from the nest made for a mighty tasty meal that evening. My family ate like kings."

WHISKEY AND THE SNAKE

The old fisherman was killing time, waiting for the evening bite. He sat in the shade of a willow tree and spun an interesting yarn.

"One time I was fishing on Whiskey Creek, named on account of the time a freight wagon, loaded with whiskey barrels, overturned at the crossing. The barrels broke apart in the rapids. The rattlesnakes in that part of the country were drunk for two weeks, or so they said.

"But anyway, after an hour of fishing without a strike I decided to look around for live bait. Hoping to find some grubs or maybe a cricket, I kicked over a log and a rattlesnake made his presence known. He was a big one and it so happened he was in the process of swallowing a frog.

"I got to wondering about the rumors of the rattlesnakes' fondness for whiskey and decided to see for myself. Now, I always carry a pint of spirits on my person and I poured a little into a hollow spot on a rock. Quick as a wink that rattlesnake let go of the frog, slithered over and started lapping whiskey like a thirsty dog drinks water on a hot day.

"I picked up the frog, worked him onto my hook and made a cast. The bait drifted a few feet and bang-go! I caught a twenty-inch rainbow. No sooner had I landed it than I began to wonder where I was gonna find another frog.

"I felt a sharp tap on my boot, looked down and that dang snake was there with another frog. He looked at me with these big pleading eyes. I pour more whiskey onto the rock and he immediately let go of the frog.

"That day I caught one fish after another until the contents of my flask was empty. And then I got the heck out of there because there is nothing worse than a rattlesnake that has had too much to drink."

SOAP 'N' WATER

Old bachelors are notorious for their housekeeping. Charlie Doak was a perfect example.

Charlie had a little cabin at the head of a draw, perched on a rimrock outcropping along a seldom-used trail. Whenever anyone passed that way Charlie would beseech them to stop and visit.

One traveler told this tale about Charlie. "He was out there waving his hat at me, calling to me when I was still a mile away. It wasn't like I could avoid the old fellow because the trail goes right up the draw past his cabin.

"I wanted to keep on going and camp on top, by the spring in the timber, but Charlie was insistent. He claimed he hadn't had anybody to talk to in a month of Sundays. Feeling sorry for the old fellow, I agreed to shoot the breeze with him for a while.

"We end up on the front porch drinking moonshine out of a jug. It tastes pretty darn good. Old Charlie makes decent shine, I will say that for him.

"Finally Charlie jumps up and dashes inside saying he's going to fix me something to eat. I tell him not to bother. Not that I couldn't use a bite to tide me over but it was just that there was no way in the world I was setting foot inside that cabin. The smell from where I sat was bad enough.

"Presently Charlie comes out, carrying a plate heaped high with steak and scrambled eggs. I want to make sure and so I ask, 'Is this plate clean?'

"Charlie answers proudly, 'Yes sir, just as clean as Soap 'n' Water can get it.'

"I finish the meal, compliment Charlie on his cooking, take another pull off the bottle and prepare myself to leave. About then this mangy dog drags himself out from under the porch. I ask what his name is and Charlie replies, 'I call him ol' Soap 'n' Water'."

PERFECTLY MATCHED

Indian Bill was a well-respected horseman and each year brought his best to the fair to compete in three days of racing. One year he ran a white horse in the first race. It looked as if it could run but came in dead last. Indian Bill was very vocal, saying the horse was his favorite and that he did not have the heart to tell it how much it had disgraced him.

At last he declared, "I run him tomorrow. He run better."

But the following race produced the same result. The white horse ran hard but was outclassed. This devastated Indian Bill and he walked around slumped-shouldered. Even his braids seemed to hang limp and dejected.

He approached a group of bettors. One of the men looked up and mocked, "I thought that horse could run. He couldn't beat a crippled duck in a footrace to a feed trough." The men laughed and puffed on their fat cigars.

"He run good," said Indian Bill.

"Better tell him that," jeered one of the men.

Indian Bill pulled his shoulders back, stood tall and told the men that he had utmost faith in his horse; that he was not only going to race the horse again but vowed it would win. To back up his boast he pulled a wad of cash from his pocket and promised to bet every dollar on his horse. The men fought to get a piece of the action.

The following day, as the white horse crossed the finish line, Indian Bill was so far ahead that he turned in the saddle to see what was keeping the other horses. He scooped up his winnings and returned to the reservation. Although no one ever knew for sure, it was suspected that there were two perfectly matched horses in his stable, one could run and one could not.

TOBACCO

"I was a sickly child," recalled 83-year-old Ed Carr. "Back in those days about all a doctor did was stroke his whiskers, look at you like a wise owl and dispense medicine that tasted twice as bad as whatever ailed you.

"My problem was my stomach. They treated me with calomel, quinine and indigo. But they did no good. I was nothing but a bag of bones.

"Then a new doctor moved into the neighborhood. He tried this and that and finally confided to Father, 'I'm stumped. I thought I could cure your boy. There is only one remedy I haven't tried.'

"Father said, 'For heaven sakes, try it.'

"'If it doesn't cure him it'll likely kill him.'

"Father replied, 'If he keeps going like he is, he's gonna die anyway. We got nothin' to lose by tryin'.'

"I was four years old at the time. But I well remember the cure. Father handed me a lit pipe filled with strong tobacco, told me to commence smoking. The smoke dang near strangled me but, by golly, I stayed with it.

"Presently I was staggering and it seemed as if everything in sight was whirling around me. I lay down in front of the fireplace and the deathly pallor of my face and my cold sweats alarmed Father. He thought I was dying.

"But I did not and several days later he had me take another dose of medicine. When I touched the pipe I began shivering and shaking, but like a man I puffed away and, strange as it may seem, that time I felt no ill effects. And in the days and weeks that followed I gained weight and was soon as husky as any lad my age.

"From the time I first smoked until now I have never had a recurrence of misery in my stomach. I truly do believe that tobacco saved my life."

PEGLEG

The homesteader was getting acquainted with a neighbor who had recently moved in on an adjoining homestead. A jug of moonshine appeared. The homesteader wet his lips with moonshine and began telling this story.

"Back in the early days, when the country was fresh and new, a man living out by himself could get awful lonesome. Pets were at a premium. The first pet I ever owned was a wild animal, to be specific a young bobcat.

"Happened to catch it in a steel trap and by the time I got to him his leg was in terrible shape. Didn't have the heart to kill him and so I packed him home. It soon became evident that if the feline's life was to be saved I was going to have to amputate the leg. Which I did.

"I nursed that critter back to health. He and I became best friends and I took to calling him Bob. Well, after Bob had recovered I saw the difficulty he had in attempting to get around on only three legs. I whittled him a wooden leg out of a chunk of hard hickory. Fastened it on with a belt-like contraption and, by golly, before long Bob was nearly as good as new. He showed his gratefulness in a variety of ways. For one, he took to sleeping curled up in a ball at the foot of my bed.

"One night I heard a strange and irregular tapping noise that emanated from the kitchen. I could not feel Bob in his customary spot and went to investigate. I tiptoed across the room and peeked into the kitchen. A shaft of moonlight illuminated Bob, poised over a small hole in the floor. His wooden leg was raised and each time a mouse appeared from the hole Bob knocked it over the head with his wooden leg. With the mystery solved I went back to bed. In the morning there were 14 dead mice."

SNAKE CHASE

"Any rattlesnakes around these parts?" inquired the traveler.

"Some. Used ta be more," stated the western storyteller. "I remember one time I was horseback, riding along the canyon, and happened to come in contact with the biggest dang rattlesnake I ever laid eyes on. Was as round as my waist and every bit of fifteen feet long. I ain't exaggerating.

"I must have woke him up from a nap because he was mad as all get out, red tongue darting in and out. It was plain to see he was fixing to strike, so I wheeled my horse and laid the spurs to him.

"Looking back over my shoulder I watched that big snake give chase, matching us stride for stride, and just for meanness taking nips at the flying hooves of my mount. We made it to the bottom of the canyon and on the flat we gained a little ground. Up ahead was my cabin and when we got there I pulled back hard on the reins, hit the ground running, just managing to make it through the door and slamming it shut behind me.

"That door was made out of a single piece of juniper, six inches thick and solid as a slab of granite. Well sir, that snake he gets to the door, rears his head back and strikes. He hits it so hard his fangs come clean through and stick out into the room a couple inches. I grab up a hammer and bend over the fangs so he can't pull back.

"Was that snake ever upset! Ooee, shook the cabin like an earthquake and rattled his tail so hard the sky was fooled into thinking there was a storm and it started in raining. But the worst part of it was my cabin didn't have windows and no back door. I sure as heck wasn't gonna open the front door."

"What did you finally do?" inquired the traveler.

The storyteller looked straight ahead, dryly answered, "Well sir, I stayed where I was and done starved to death."

THE BRAG

Three old timers were sitting on the bench in front of the drug store swapping yarns. The best bragger of the bunch claimed, "Luckiest day I ever had was in '38. Take that back, we had the big flood in '38. It was '39. "Had me a muzzleloader. Big old thing. I used to shove my corncob pipe in the end of the barrel to keep dirt from getting inside. The day I'm remembering I spotted a dandy elk on the opposite side of the river. He had come down for a drink. In my excitement to shoot I forgot to take the corncob pipe out of the barrel. When I touched her off the barrel exploded and metal flew in all directions.

"It just so happened that a flock of geese was flying overhead and I killed six of them with shrapnel as well as a pair of mallards that were floating past at the time. Besides that, the explosion knocked me back and I stepped on a pheasant which in turn scared the beejeebers out of me and I lost my balance and fell in the river. When I came up I had something flopping around inside my shirt and discovered I had netted eleven catfish and a snapping turtle.

"On the far side of the river the corn cob pipe had gone completely through the elk and managed to kill a pair of spotted owls sitting side by side in a snag. When they fell dead the snag toppled over and broke apart a bees nest. Honey ran into the river, making the water so sweet all the fish got toothaches and came to the surface and I scooped them up free for the taking."

"Never heard you tell that one before," said one of the men in surprise.

"Would have told it sooner," said the bragger, "but I didn't have a hunting or fishing license. I was waiting for the statute of limitations to run out."

STAKING A CLAIM

The homesteader was explaining to a newcomer the process he went through in staking his first donation land claim. He declared, "Back in those days there wasn't a surveyor west of the Mississippi River. I realized that platting the land was going to take a little Yankee ingenuity.

"The first thing I did was climb a high point to get a lay of the territory. From there I could see what this land had in the way of possibilities. I began to formulate my plan to have an efficient farming and ranching operation.

"My reasoning in choosing this spot was that I needed acreage in the river bottom for farming. The soil there was deep and rich and the water table high. In order to build a house and barn I needed lumber. There was a good stand of trees in the mountains. I vowed to have some timberland. And I wanted plenty of range so my stock would have room to graze.

"With that criteria in mind I went far out on the plain and drove a stake into the virgin ground. And then, after taking a deep breath, I started running and I did not stop until I was forced to take another breath. Here I drove a second stake. From this point I gauged a right angle, took another deep breath and ran until I was out of air. I repeated this procedure until the four sides were staked.

"I soon saw the error of my ways because upon measuring distance I discovered the legs across the plain were a uniform twenty miles. But the one going into the mountains was only ten miles and the one coming downhill was thirty miles in length. However, I was able to rectify my mistake by plowing a furrow around the perimeter and then taking hold of the short side and pulling the excess from the long side. This squared my land claim."

Rick Steber's *Tales of the Wild West* series is available in hardbound books ($14.95) and paperback books ($4.95) featuring illustrations by Don Gray; as well as in cassette tapes ($7.95) narrated by Dallas McKennon. Current titles in the series include:

❏	Vol. 1	*Oregon Trail*
❏	Vol. 2	*Pacific Coast*
❏	Vol. 3	*Indians*
❏	Vol. 4	*Cowboys*
❏	Vol. 5	*Women of the West*
❏	Vol. 6	*Children's Stories*
❏	Vol. 7	*Loggers*
❏	Vol. 8	*Mountain Men*
❏	Vol. 9	*Miners*
❏	Vol. 10	*Grandpa's Stories*
❏	Vol. 11	*Pioneers*
❏	Vol. 12	*Campfire Stories*
❏	Vol. 13	*Tall Tales*

Other books written by Rick Steber include *Roundup, Oregon Trail—Last of the Pioneers, Heartwood, New York to Nome, Wild Horse Rider, Where Rolls the Oregon, Traces,* and *Rendezvous.* Ask your local retailer about Rick Steber's books or request a free catalog with a complete listing from:

Bonanza Publishing
Box 204
Prineville, Oregon 97754

Saddle Ranch Elementary
805 English Sparrow Trail
Highlands Ranch, CO 80126